D1140616

THE COMPLETE BEGINNER'S GUIDE TO

Watercolour

THE COMPLETE BEGINNER'S GUIDE TO

Watercolour

Bath New York Singapore Hong Kong Cologne Delhi Melbourne

This edition published by Parragon in 2009

Parragon

Queen Street House

4 Queen Street

Bath BA1 1HE, UK

Copyright © Parragon Books Ltd 2004

All rights reserved. No part of this publication may

be reproduced, stored in a retrieval system, or

transmitted, in any form or by any means, electronic,

mechanical, photocopying, recording or otherwise,

without the prior permission of the copyright holder.

This edition designed by Design Principals

Drawings by Terry Longhurst

Text by Angela Gair and Theodora Philcox

Edited by Susie Johns and Theodora Philcox

ISBN: 978-1-4075-7437-0

Printed in Malaysia

Contents

Introduction

Drawing and painting are two of the first skills we develop as children. Through them we communicate, express our feelings, and often just simply enjoy the wonder of colour.

Although one of our earliest skills, and despite the fact that the world we inhabit is overwhelmingly full of visual imagery, our culture gives priority to the spoken and written word. Before we know it, we lose the freedom with which we drew as a child and we can become embarrassed at our apparent incompetence. Many of us just give up, only later to wish that we could do it! The good news is that we can. Given time and practise, everyone can draw and paint, and this book is intended to show you how.

Watercolour is the oldest of all paint media and it remains the most popular. Over the centuries it has been prized for its luminosity and fluidity of application, making it the ideal choice for spontaneous colour studies, particularly for capturing the transient qualities of light and colour in nature. Furthermore, it has the ability to achieve results that range from the strikingly vibrant to the subtle and delicate, making it suitable for a wide range of painting styles. Whilst not necessarily the easiest of materials to use, it requires little equipment; it's clean; and at its simplest, starts with those techniques we learned in childhood.

A successful painting is largely dependent on a sound drawing, and this book teaches both in tandem. It will take you through the basics of rendering form through contour and tone; how to create an interesting composition and how to cope with perspective. Once you have grasped the fundamentals, you will have the confidence

to allow your natural creativity to take over and you can begin to forge your own path, bend the rules a little and discover your own unique way of representing the world.

Like any skill, the ability to draw and paint successfully doesn't develop overnight. You will need to learn how to 'look', and then practise and practise. Make quick sketches as you sit in a park or café; draw your family or pets as they work or relax around your home; visit galleries, and study paintings and illustrations in books and magazines. Gradually you will begin to see like an artist and the results may well surprise you!

Getting Started

The pencil is the most familiar, natural drawing instrument. It is also the most versatile, capable of producing an infinite range of lines and marks. Pencil drawings can be done using lines alone, or by using tone alone without lines, or any number of techniques in between.

The quality of a pencil line can be varied by the grade of pencil chosen, its sharpness, the way it is held, the degree of pressure applied, and the texture of the paper surface. Drawing pencils come in several grades, 'H' denoting hard and 'B' denoting soft. The HB (medium grade) is a good all-rounder, while an 8B (very soft) will give you a wide range of linear and tonal effects. Hard leads are suitable for precise lines and details, but in general they are less versatile than the soft leads.

You will have also used coloured pencils whilst at school. There is no reason why you shouldn't try using these for ordinary drawings as well as for a colouring material.

They're very useful for sketching, as they are clean and very portable, allowing you to add touches of colour without the fuss of water or other equipment. The more expensive pencils have lovely soft 'leads' that will blend and give the tonal range of graphite pencils. Buy the pencils individually and try different brands to see which suit you best. You can also buy water-soluble coloured pencils that bridge the gap between drawing and painting. You can achieve a wide range of effects with these, and they offer the ultimate in flexibility when painting on the move.

There is a wide range of other drawing media you can experiment with. Charcoal, the traditional medium of artists, encourages you to make broad, fluid strokes, and can be easily erased if you make a mistake.

Pastels offer the control of a pencil combined with the intensity and blending capacity of paint, but buy your pastels with care, as some are much harder than others. Oil pastels make thick buttery marks, and also have great intensity of colour, but they are harder to blend, and can produce cruder, harsh results. Many artists like to combine pen and washes of ink, either using a traditional dip pen or the more modern felt tip or technical pen. In this way spontaneous loose or detailed images can be enhanced with tonal development.

Across history artists have used anything and everything that can make a mark for drawing. Experiment; only be limited by your imagination.

Pencils can make a wide range of marks from single lines to tonal areas created by blending soft pencil with a finger or cloth. Experiment using different grades of pencil and using them on their sides to make broad strokes, or their points to create textural marks. Cross-hatching can be sparse or dense to create varied areas of shadow.

Watercolours

Watercolours can be bought in pans (small slabs of solid paint), or tubes either singly or in pre-selected sets. You can also buy watercolours in two grades – artists' and student quality. Artists' quality paints contain higher concentrations of quality pigment, and will provide stronger, more luminous and transparent colour than student quality paints.

Many artists advise you to start with the best quality paints you can afford to give you the best chance of success, but you might feel inhibited using expensive pigments during your early experiments. Try both, and compare for yourself. As with all art materials, try different brands too. There really is a difference between them.

Different types of paper will give you different results. You can use any type of paper for sketching, but there are special papers for watercolour that you can choose from that give excellent results. Cold-pressed paper (also referred to as 'Not', because it is not hot-pressed!), has a semi-rough surface, takes a smooth wash well, and is also good for detail. Alternatively rough paper has a more defined surface, or 'tooth', to hold the paint. This paper creates a more textured result as paint either settles in the hollows, or skates over the top, leaving flecks of white. Of the two, cold-pressed paper is the most versatile and easier for the beginner to handle. The third type, hot-pressed paper has a hard smooth surface which means paint tends to slide off it. It is great for detailed work, but not a good choice for fluid painting. Paper comes in various weights. To prevent buckling when using water, a paper of more than 140lb/300gsm should be used. Lighter papers can be stretched on a board to ensure they stay flat.

Brushes

Buy the best brushes you can afford as they will not only last a long time, but really help you achieve good results. They should be able to hold a lot of paint, and allow you to release it steadily. They should also be springy and give a good point or edge that can create a crisp mark when required. Kolinsky sable is definitely the best choice, even though it is expensive. There are alternatives such as the cheaper red or pure sable, or squirrel. However, if you prefer not to use products from animals, there are some excellent synthetic brushes on the market.

Eventually you will need a range of brushes, but to start with the most useful will be a round brush which can be used for broad washes as well as for fine detail. A set including sizes 3, 5 and 12 will take you a long way. Later you could add a fine rigger brush for detail and fine lines, and a mop, wash or flat brush to assist in laying in large areas of colour or broad washes.

Stretching Paper

When paper gets wet, the fibres swell, causing the surface to warp and cockle. This can make it difficult to work on, with colour pooling in the recesses. Even once the painting is finished and dry, it never returns to its original state. Any paper that is less than 140lb/300gsm needs to be stretched before you start painting.

Stretching paper is a simple process whereby the paper is pre-wetted, and taped to a board. As the paper dries, it contracts, creating a smooth working surface. Paper that is less than 140lb/300gsm is likely to buckle or warp when water is added, unless it is stretched.

You will need:

• A sheet of watercolour paper

• A drawing board bigger than your paper

• Gummed brown tape about 3" (10 cm) wide

• Two sponges (one for wetting the tape, the other for smoothing the paper).

1. Cut four strips of gummed brown tape, one for each side of the piece of paper. Cut these slightly longer than the sides. Put them to one side for the moment.

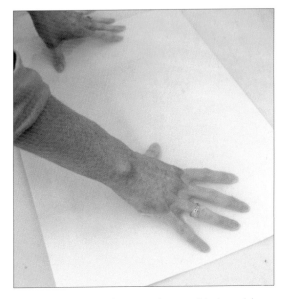

2. Soak a sheet of paper thoroughly in cold water for two or three minutes, (longer, if the paper is heavier), perhaps in the bath. This is to allow the fibres in the paper to expand.

3. Lift the paper and gently shake off the excess water. Place it on a drawing board, which must be lying flat. If you are using a bath, the board can be laid across the top.

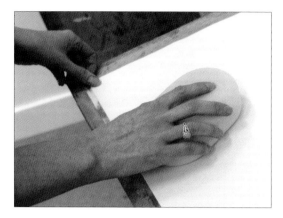

4. Smooth the paper out with a clean sponge or your fingers. It probably won't be perfectly smooth at this stage, but don't worry; when it dries it will be tight.

6. Tape down the other sides in the same way as before.

7. You can mop up excess moisture with a damp sponge, but then leave to dry for several hours, flat, and away from direct heat. As the water evaporates, the fibres in the paper contract, leaving the paper tight and smooth. If it dries out too quickly, it can either pull the tape off the board or split, so don't be tempted to use a hairdryer!

8. Only when you have completed your painting and it is totally dry should you remove the paper from the board by cutting it along its edges with a knife.

Tips:

1. Use different coloured sponges so you don't confuse them.

2. Only use cold water for soaking your paper. Hot water can remove the sizing from the paper leaving it too absorbent and unworkable.

5. Moisten a strip of gummed tape with your second sponge and stick it down firmly along one side of the paper with about one third of the tape on the paper, and two-thirds on the board. This will stop the paper pulling off the board. If you use the same sponge for wetting the gummed tape as for smoothing the paper, you might leave a non-absorbent gum residue on your painting surface.

Washes and Techniques

Colour washes form the basis of watercolour painting. They are thin layers of paint heavily diluted to maximise transparency. The following three pages describe and show a range of washes and painting techniques that, once you have practised and mastered them, will become the methods you use most to produce your pictures.

It is important to keep your paints fluid and transparent, and the colours bright and fresh: you need to use plenty of clean water and rinse your brushes thoroughly after each colour application. Try not to 'muddy' the image with too many colours and keep reworking to a minimum to maintain the delicacy of the washes. Take the time to plan the sequence of washes you are going to use and apply them quickly and decisively.

The traditional watercolour technique is to work from light to dark, establishing the basic forms and local colours with thin, broad washes. Apply the mid-tones, then the darkest tones, waiting for each area to dry before you add another wash.

Wet in wet painting is one of the key techniques of watercolour. Diluted paint can be applied either to damp paper, or added to another area of paint that is still wet. The colours will run into each other forming soft blends.

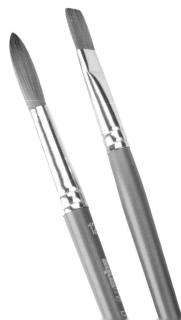

A flat wash uses one colour evenly across the paper. It can be achieved by wetting the paper, and then drawing a brush loaded with dilute paint across the area in a single stroke. This is then repeated again and again down the paper, with each stroke slightly overlapping the one above to pick up and blend with the wet edge.

Flat Wash

Graded Wash

Variegated Wash

Graded washes are achieved in the same way as a flat wash except that each stroke is more diluted than the last.

Variegated washes use two or more colours. Once the first part of the wash has been applied using one of the colours, the brush is washed and then applies the next colour, partly overlapping the original colour, and blending wet in wet.

Wet on dry

Glazing

Painting wet on dry allows for sharp edges in a painting. If thin washes of colour are painted over one that is dry, interesting transparent blends are achieved, resulting in stronger yet luminous colour. This technique is known as glazing.

Lifting out

Sponging

Paint can be applied with a sponge either to create washes or to produce textured areas depending on how dilute the paint is. Dry or damp sponges can also be used for lifting colour out. Colour can be lifted out to create soft highlights or clouds. Kitchen paper can also be used for this.

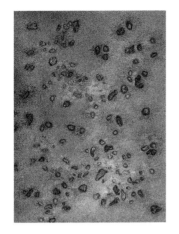

Salt

Salt

If rock salt is scattered over a wet area of paint, the crystals will absorb the paint. Once the paint is absolutely dry the crystals can be brushed off leaving a variety of patterns depending on the grade of salt.

Scraffito means 'scratched off'. When the paint is dry or nearly dry it is possible to drag a sharp implement such as your fingernail, a blade, or even the end of a brush through the surface, lifting the paint off in sharp lines.

If you draw a candle across your paper and then paint over it, the wax will resist the paint, leaving an interesting broken texture suitable for walls or rocks.

Scratching out/Scraffito

Wax resist

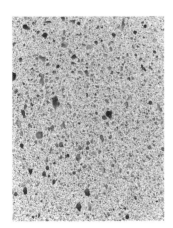

Spattering

Interesting textures can be achieved by spattering paint with a toothbrush or even using a spray device. Dip the toothbrush into the paint and then draw either your thumb or a piece of card swiftly across the bristles, and the paint will flick in small droplets onto your painting. Mask off any areas you don't want affected.

Fine Spattering

Colour

Colour can be used not only to describe objects, but also to suggest mood and atmosphere. The colour wheel will help you to understand how colour works and enable you to use it expressively in your paintings.

The core colours are the three primaries – red, yellow, and blue – so called because they cannot be mixed from other colours. These are linked by the secondary colours, which are each mixed from two primaries: red and yellow make orange, yellow and blue make green, red and blue make violet.

Colours that are next to each other on the wheel are described as harmonious because they share a common base colour. Harmonious colours create a unified image with no jarring notes. Pairs of colours that are opposite each other on the wheel are known as complementary pairs. When placed side by side they intensify each other, thus a patch of red looks more vibrant when juxtaposed with green.

One half of the wheel comprises warm colours – reds, oranges, and yellows – and the other comprises cool blues, greens, and violets. Because warm colours appear to advance and cool colours to recede, the use of warm hues in the foreground and cool ones in the background accentuates the illusion of depth and atmosphere in landscape paintings.

The colour wheel is a simplified version of the colours of the spectrum, formed into a circle. It is a handy reference for understanding the way colours relate to each other. The arrangement of colours on the wheel shows the relationship between the primary colours and their opposite, or complementary colours, and their adjacent colours.

Colours that lie opposite each other on the colour wheel are called complementary colours. When a colour and its complementary are placed next to each other they intensify each other; when mixed together they neutralise each other.

Drawing Simple Shapes and Rendering Form

The most basic forms to be found in nature – the cube, the sphere, the cone, and the cylinder – can be used to simplify your understanding of any object you paint, no matter how complex.

When you come to paint complicated subjects – the human figure, buildings and trees in landscape, fruits and flowers in a still life – it helps to visualise them first as simple geometric shapes. All the objects around us are combinations of the curves and planes found in the sphere, the cone, the cylinder, and the cube. A building is basically a cube; most fruits and vegetables are roughly spherical; a bottle and a tree trunk are basically cylinders; poplar trees are conical in shape, as are some flower heads. Learning to see objects in terms of simple shapes that can then be broken down into smaller, more complex shapes, helps us to paint them more easily and accurately.

The difference between flat, two-dimensional shapes and solid, three-dimensional forms is the way light falls on objects, creating shadows, half-tones and highlights that reveal their planes and surfaces. In painting, this is represented using tone and shading – in other words, degrees of light and dark.

Any shape in nature, from a flower right up to a mountain, can be worked out in simple three-dimensional terms. It was the great artist Cézanne who said, "Treat nature in terms of the cylinder, the sphere, the cone…"

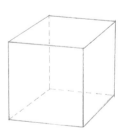

These four geometric shapes are the main basic forms to be found in nature and can be used to simplify your understanding of any subject, from a flower to a human figure.

Practise modelling form by drawing outlines of the four basic shapes and then converting them into objects by filling in the outlines with tone.

On rounded objects the tone changes are gradual, following the curve of the surface as it turns away from the light. The highlight is at the point nearest to the light source.

Apply charcoal to the darkest part of the sphere and blend it with your finger to show how it curves towards the light. An eraser can be used to pull out highlights and reflected light.

On rounded forms, the shadow side may lighten slightly near the outer edge. This is caused by light being reflected back onto the object by nearby surfaces.

Where edges are sharp, as in the cube, there are clearly defined planes of light and shadow.

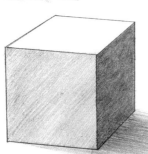

Tone can be built up in line. Using a pencil or pen and ink, try hatching and cross-hatching, increasing the density where the shadows are deepest.

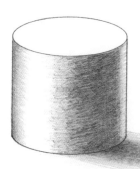

Cast shadows vary in size, tone and shape according to the angle and distance of the light source.

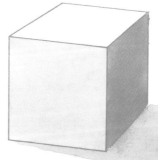

Use a pen to draw a cube and then fill in the shadow planes with a brush and diluted ink. Build up the darkest tone with overlaid washes.

Contour Shapes

An outline is a flat shape that describes only two dimensions. A contour drawing describes all three dimensions – length, width, and depth – because it follows the bumps and hollows within the form.

Drawing most often involves using line to describe the three-dimensional quality of an object. The line must describe the bulk of the form and not just its outline. If you draw the outline of a figure, for example, it looks flat, like a cartoon character. There is no information in the drawing to tell us that the arms, legs, and so on are actually rounded. But as soon as you work across the drawing with a few simple contour lines that describe the bumps and hollows created by the bones and muscles, the way the hair lies, and the creases in the clothing, the figure becomes solid and three-dimensional – even without shading.

A contour drawing is rather like a contour map: it travels across the forms, indicating where the surface of the object is close to us or further away, where it is curved and where it is flat. By making subtle changes in the width and weight of the lines you can also describe the fullness and 'weight' of the forms.

The best way to describe objects accurately and make them look convincingly three-dimensional is to draw them as

This outline drawing conveys very little information about the three-dimensional qualities of the forms, so they look flat.

Here, contour lines are introduced which map out the curvature of the apples, explaining their forms.

though they are transparent. By drawing both what is seen and what is hidden, you don't just describe the outer shape of an object, you get a better sense of its underlying structure and this helps you to draw it more accurately. You can rub out any unwanted lines later if you want to, though they often add 'texture' to a drawing.

This method is especially useful when drawing cylindrical objects like cups, bowls and vases. If you draw the entire base of the object, and not just the bit you can see at the front, it will appear solid and planted squarely on the surface. You will find it much easier to draw the elliptical shape of the opening accurately, too.

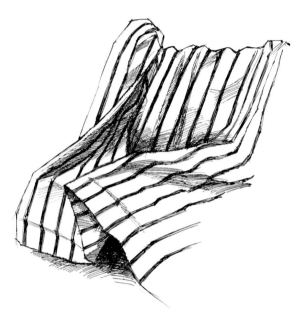

If you drape a piece of striped fabric and then draw it by copying the stripes, you will see how the stripes become contour lines that describe the three-dimensional curves and folds in the fabric.

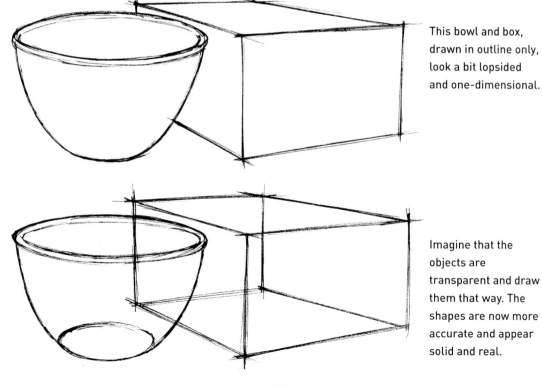

This bowl and box, drawn in outline only, look a bit lopsided and one-dimensional.

Imagine that the objects are transparent and draw them that way. The shapes are now more accurate and appear solid and real.

Simple Perspective

*P*erspective is a system used by artists to create a convincing illusion of three-dimensional form and space on a flat piece of paper. The basic principles are very straightforward.

Before you can paint anything in perspective, you must first establish the horizon line. If you can't see the actual horizon (in a town, for instance), just remember that the horizon is at your own eye level. The horizon level will change according to whether you are sitting down or standing up but it is always directly in front of your eye.

Vanishing points

The basic assumption of perspective is that parallel horizontal lines that recede into the distance appear to converge at a single point on the horizon, at the centre of vision. This is called the vanishing point. All lines above your eye level will slant down to the vanishing point and lines below your eye level will slant up to the vanishing point.

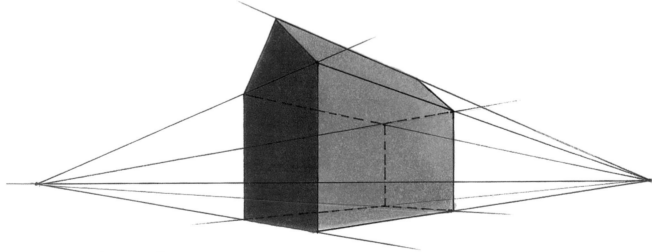

Two-point perspective
Each side of this house is seen at an angle of roughly 45 degrees to the picture plane. Each side appears to recede towards a vanishing point on the horizon line on the left and right of the image. To draw the building, start with the nearest vertical line and assess the angles at which the sides of the building recede from it. Extend these lines to the vanishing points. Using this framework you can now draw the windows and doors in perspective.

One and two-point perspective

One-point perspective refers to a situation where there is only one vanishing point at the centre line of vision. However, objects are often viewed from an oblique angle. If you are drawing the corner of a building, for instance, you would need to plot two vanishing points, at which the converging lines of each side of the building meet.

With two-point perspective it is likely that at least one vanishing point, and sometimes both, will be outside the picture area. You have to imagine the vanishing points in the space beyond your page and estimate the angles of the building by eye.

[1] To draw a row of arches or windows in perspective, showing how they appear to narrow as they recede, first plot the horizon line and the lines of the top and bottom of the building converging towards the vanishing point.

[2] Draw a line from halfway up the first upright to the vanishing point. Draw in the second upright. Take a diagonal line from the top of the first upright through the centre of the second. Where it meets the base line, position the third upright. Repeat until you reach the end of the building.

When drawing figures which are receding into the distance, plot converging lines from the nearest figure to the vanishing point. You can then draw the distant figures to the correct size in relation to the foreground figure.

Aerial Perspective and Viewpoint

Aerial perspective is a further development of linear perspective. This term describes a natural optical illusion caused by the presence of water vapour and dust particles in the atmosphere. These affect visibility, making colours, tone and forms appear less distinct the further away they are. The most effective means of creating the illusion of depth in your paintings, particularly in landscapes, is by using tone and colour to recreate the effects of aerial perspective.

Imagine that you are standing in a field with the landscape stretching away as far as the eye can see. As your eye travels from the foreground to the horizon you will notice that colours which appear warm and bright close up gradually become cooler, paler, and bluer as they recede towards the horizon. Tones and tonal contrast appear strongest in the foreground and become progressively weaker in the distance. Texture and detail also become less distinct the further away they are. To create the illusion of deep space in your landscape paintings, all you have to do is to mimic these effects, making your tones and colour fade gradually towards the horizon.

A useful tip for representing the effects of aerial perspective in monochrome is to visualise the landscape almost as a series of vertical, receding planes. The foreground plane is strongest in tone and detail; the middle ground and background planes become progressively paler and less distinct as they get closer to the horizon.

Placing the horizon

Take time to observe your subject from different viewpoints and to make several sketches of it. You will be surprised how even small changes of viewpoint can dramatically alter the perspective and the impression of depth in the scene. The sketches here demonstrate how altering the horizon can create a very different sense of space, and add drama if positioned either very high or very low.

An imaginative viewpoint can make for a more striking image. Looking at the landscape from a high viewpoint is fascinating because it is relatively unfamiliar. Why not climb up to the top of a hill and sketch the scene rolled out before you.

In landscapes, placing the horizon in the centre of the paper has the effect of dividing the composition in two, leaving the eye undecided where to go. It is best to place it a little above or below centre so that you can emphasise either the foreground or the sky.

Looking at a scene from a low viewpoint also offers a fresh perspective on the landscape. If you position yourself at the bottom of a slope, for instance, a building at the top of the slope will tower dramatically above the horizon line.

Composition

When you begin a painting, the first thing to consider is the composition. Good composition means arranging the elements in your subject to create an appealing and well-balanced drawing that attracts and holds the viewer's attention.

It is important that the centre of interest is positioned with care. Never place it in the middle of the picture as this produces a static arrangement; position it off-centre so as to create a visual tension that gives a more lively effect. The rule of thirds is a good guideline to follow. Also, avoid having two objects of equal interest in a drawing as they will vie for attention; if a scene contains two trees, for example, make one bigger than the other, of a different tone, or push one further back.

The secondary elements in the painting should be arranged so as to take the eye on a gentle journey from foreground to background, or from one object to another. Look for lines or implied lines that follow through the picture and link one area to another, such as a meandering road or river curving up through the scene, or the contours of cloud formations, or even shadows cast on the ground.

This landscape format drawing is divided horizontally and vertically into thirds. Both the jug and the vase of flowers align with the vertical thirds. The points where objects overlap, such as the vase and bowls, are positioned close to where lines intersect.

This portrait format still life is again divided into horizontal and vertical thirds. The vase sits on the intersecting vertical on the right and the flowers fall mostly within the upper horizontal third, balanced by the bowls of fruit in the lower third.

The composition should appear balanced and harmonious, while containing enough variety to entertain the eye. For example, the rounded forms of fruits, flowers, jugs and bowls in a still life repeat and echo each other, creating a satisfying harmony; at the same time, visual interest is achieved through varying their shapes, sizes, colours, and tones.

The sketches shown opposite demonstrate traditional methods of dividing up the picture area to achieve a balanced design. The 'rule of thirds' is a simple mathematical formula based on the principles of harmony and proportion. Imagine the picture area divided into thirds, horizontally and vertically; any strong horizontal or vertical elements in the sketches should coincide with these lines, and the points where two lines intersect are good places to locate the focal point of the drawing.

This Japanese bonsai tree creates a pleasing curvilinear composition. The outline of the tree fits loosely within a circle and the eye naturally follows the twists and curves of the branches up, around and down.

Arrangements based on an underlying geometric shape break up the picture in a pleasing way. Here, a still life is loosely grouped within the shape of an equilateral triangle. This construction has a natural stability, enhanced by grouping the objects so that they overlap each other.

Make sure that your focus of interest is placed off-centre. Here the curved path draws the eye to the focal point, which is located at the intersection of thirds.

Using a Viewfinder

*I*t can sometimes be difficult to decide what to draw when confronted with a landscape. Start by taking a walk around with your sketchbook and a cardboard viewfinder and note down anything that grabs your attention. From any one position there may be several directions of view that offer subjects to draw. A viewfinder will help you isolate a particular section of a subject.

With practice, a viewfinder will help to train your eye to see potential subjects and to compose them well. When the scene is concentrated within the window of the frame, you can see at a glance how it will look on paper. Bring the viewfinder closer to your eye to include a wide-angle view; hold it away from you to select a small area. Raise or lower it to alter the position of the horizon line, depending on whether you want to emphasise the sky or the landscape features. Don't forget the rule of thirds, many landscape paintings are divided into one-third sky, two-thirds land (or vice versa); no one quite knows why, but the human eye finds that this proportion has a pleasing balance. And remember too, don't just look at your subject horizontally; you can turn the viewfinder upright and work with it in a vertical format to good effect.

You can make a viewfinder by cutting a window measuring about 10 x 15 cm from the centre of a piece of card. Hold it up at arm's length, close one eye, and move your arm back and forth and left to right until the scene sits happily in the 'window'.

With the horizontal (landscape) format the eye can roam from side to side and the mood is one of calm and restfulness.

With the upright (portrait) format the vertical elements become more dominant. The mood becomes more enclosed and intimate.

This sketch conveys a strong sense of space on a small scale by means of both the sharp perspective of the centrally placed road and the set-back position of the focal point.

Landscapes

There is no doubt that landscape is the most popular subject for drawing and painting. Apart from the wealth of material to inspire you – you can choose anything from a few leaves to a panoramic vista of trees, fields and sky – there is the added delight of being in the countryside 'communing with nature'.

The ever-changing sea is a more challenging prospect for the artist. Waves, foam, breakers and swells require a great deal of patience and experience to capture. However, beach scenes and harbour scenes are excellent subjects to start off with. As with landscapes, you can choose to home in on just one element, such as people on the beach, cliffs and dunes, boats or boatyards. Here, the sea just becomes part of the scene and is easier to deal with.

Composing a Landscape

No matter how breathtaking a landscape view is, you may find that you have to select and rearrange the elements of the scene in order to create a more balanced image.

Once you have chosen a landscape view, walk around it with your viewfinder and make rapid sketches to see how the composition looks on paper. Try to forget, for the moment, about 'trees, fields and clouds' and think instead of 'lines, shapes and tones'. These elements should be arranged on the paper so that there is one main area of interest, supported by secondary features which lead the eye from the foreground, into and around the picture, eventually coming to rest at the focal point.

Start by breaking the scene down into large, simple areas based on sky, horizon and foreground. Make sure the horizon doesn't cut across the middle of the paper as this creates identical spaces on either side of it, which is boring. Position it in either the upper third of the picture or the lower,

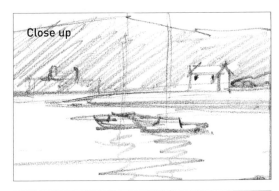

Close up

Mid-distance

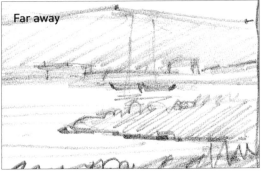

Far away

These three sketches show how even a slight change of viewpoint can alter the balance of shapes and tones, and even the mood, of the scene. A soft pencil is ideal for making thumbnail sketches because you can get down the features and the tonal areas quickly.

depending on whether you want to emphasise the sky or the land. Place the focal point somewhere off-centre, at a point that is a different distance from each edge of the paper, thus creating balance.

Try to ensure that similar shapes are echoed throughout the picture, knitting the diverse elements together. At the same time, introduce subtle contrasts that entertain the eye: angular and flowing shapes, busy areas and quiet areas, light and dark tones, bright and muted colours.

For a simple landscape, an uneven division of land and sky is usually preferable to a mid-page horizon. By making the foreground the largest area, you can add to the illusion of space and depth. Opt for a low horizon if you want to emphasise a dramatic skyline.

Natural features of the landscape often provide strong cues for the arrangement of a composition. In this sketch, the curve of the country lane sweeps down from the foreground, leading the eye into the middle distance, where it is then led upward in a criss-cross fashion by the linear patterns of fields and hedgerows to the distant hills.

Pencil Landscape

The ordinary graphite pencil has a freshness and immediacy that makes it ideal for outdoor sketching. It is very versatile, capable of suggesting light and atmosphere, space, and depth.

Make sure you choose the right grade of pencil for your sketches. An H pencil will only give a pale line, no matter how hard you press, whereas a soft pencil such as a 6B can be controlled by pressure to give lines of varying weight and thickness, as well as a wide range of tones from light to dark. Soft pencils are ideal for drawing landscapes on location. They are speedy and easy to work with, helping you to capture a scene quickly and with minimum fuss – essential when you are working outdoors in changeable conditions.

If you have access to the countryside, why not find a scene that appeals to you and spend a few hours drawing it with just a couple of pencils – say, a 2B and an 8B. A view like this one, with hills, fields, and woodland stretching to the horizon, presents a particular challenge; without the benefit of colour, you have to rely on lines and tones alone to create a sense of spatial recession.

[1] Using a 2B pencil, start by plotting the position of the horizon line. Then lightly sketch in the curve of the river, which establishes the perspective of the scene. Briefly outline the important contours of the hills, fields, and trees, remembering to make them smaller as the scene recedes towards the horizon. The whole effect should remain free and sketchy at this stage.

[2] You can now start to build up tone and detail. Use the softer 8B pencil to work gently over the darker parts of the scene with hatched lines. Vary the pressure on the pencil to create a variety of tones, and alter the direction of the strokes to capture the natural features. Don't work up any one area at a time – build up the drawing as a whole, moving freely all over the paper to ensure a harmonic result.

[3] Continue to develop the various tones and texture in the scene: use long, evenly spaced hatching for the smooth fields and short lines and scribbles for the trees. Suggest spatial recession using a progression from strong to light tones and a diminishing scale of textural marks into the distance.

Painting Trees and Foliage

Trees are likely to feature in most landscape paintings, and unless you are going for a completely stylized effect, it is helpful to gain some understanding of the basic shapes of key species. Look carefully at how branches lead off from one another, thinning out and tapering towards the boundary of the overall tree shape. You can achieve some really good results simply by making your brush or a sponge do the work.

Try to define the silhouette and 'gesture' of various tree species and compare their differences. Draw simple tonal sketches like these using a soft medium such as a graphite stick. This cherry laurel, for instance, has a squat, rounded silhouette.

Evergreen trees such as spruce, alders and cedars tend to be angular in outline, with dense masses of dark foliage.

Stippling with a fairly dry, flat brush is useful to describe a fir tree.

Here a quick pencil sketch has been enhanced with simple watercolour washes to create a lively impression of an oak tree in all its summer glory. Notice that the foliage is not a solid mass; there are lots of 'sky holes', particularly around the outer edges of the tree. Paint the sunlit foliage first, with light, warm greens. Whilst the paint is still just damp, apply successive layers of cool, dark bluish greens for the foliage in shadow.

Painting wet-in-wet quickly creates a sense of volume and shadow.

Create texture by using the tooth of the watercolour paper and dragging a dry brush over the surface.

Painting Skies and Creating Atmosphere

The mood of a sky will dramatically alter the mood of your painting. A dark stormy sky above a brilliantly lit field will make an immediate impact; multiple clouds can create rhythm and add perspective, and the effects of a setting sun can be visually magnetic.

Skies are very important as they can determine the atmosphere of the entire painting. Watercolour is a fantastic medium for painting them, its fluidity and transparency matches the qualities you are trying to create. Study skies carefully before you begin to paint them. Examine the variations in colour temperature from the sky above you to that of the horizon. Look how perspective affects the appearance of clouds as they retreat into the distance. Cloud formations change so quickly that it is useful to record them in order to develop an understanding of their structure and meaning. John Constable was amongst the first to do this and his powerful paintings bear testimony to the value of his dedicated study. In some cases the sky can be the subject of the painting, with a small strip of land merely there for context.

Mist is another way to create atmosphere in a painting, allowing areas to come in and out of focus, adding a sense of mystery and stillness to a landscape.

Soft-edged Cumulus Clouds

White fluffy cumulus clouds bring warm sunny days to mind. Set against blue skies, if observed carefully, they can create a sense of depth as their size diminishes as they recede further towards the horizon. Soft-edged cloud shapes can be created by lifting colour out from wet paint with tissues. For a harder edge, colour needs to be added to a dry surface to define distinct cloud shapes. Whatever methods you use, make sure you vary the sizes of the clouds to make them look credible.

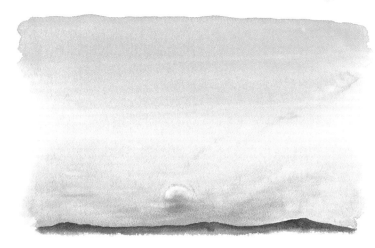

Sunrise and Sunset

There is a tendency to make sunsets, in particular, sentimental or romantic, to the detriment of capturing the true essence of the moment. Sunrise and sunset creates warm light, sometimes resulting in layers of yellow, orange or red at the horizon whilst a cool blue presides overhead. The colour combinations can be very seductive, and if storm clouds creep in overhead, the result can be extremely dramatic.

Snow

Snow clouds can be fairly flat with a touch of yellow. The snow flakes themselves can be picked out from darker clouds and the surroundings either by spattering opaque white over a dry surface, or you can preserve flecks of white with masking fluid or using the tooth of the paper.

Stormy sky

The density of storm clouds can create dramatic colour contrasts when set against a ray of light. Such skies might be composed of huge dark cumulus clouds, or heavy strata. Clouds tend to be lighter on the lower sides where the sun creeps through. This can be used to generate a sense of volume.

Painting Water

In pools, rivers, crashing waves and falls, or simply in puddles, water can add another dimension to a painting with its reflections and distortions. It tends to add a bit of life, and can provide a focal point or lead the viewer's eye around or back into the picture space.

Water will reflect the colour of the sky, making a useful visual link between the two. For the beginner it can be quite daunting to paint. The trick is to paint what you see rather than what you think you ought to see.

There are a few absolute rules. Water can never flow uphill, and ripples and waves will always be horizontal, and follow a pattern. Water also follows the rules of perspective with ripples and waves appearing smaller and closer together the further they recede into the picture.

Clouds will cast shadows on water, and thus the pattern of colour needs to match. Rocks can generate interest as waves break over them, and they can also serve to emphasize the sense of depth, leading the eye towards the horizon.

Quiet waterways generate clear reflections. Paint what you see, noting any changes in tone and which parts of the reflection are obscured by the land.

Waterfalls add drama and movement and also help to lead the eye through the picture space. Spray can be achieved through spattering or using opaque white.

Sketching and Painting on Location

Although working from photographs can be very convenient, nothing can achieve more spontaneous and dynamic results than working on location. However, many people find it very daunting for a number of reasons including the fact that the amount of detail around you can be overwhelming. It is a skill in itself to be able to simplify what you see in front of you.

Painting out of doors, unless you are in a very remote spot, is likely to attract attention. Whilst there is a social aspect to this, it is likely to distract you, either by making you self-conscious of your efforts, or just by breaking your concentration. Try to develop a friendly but thick skin with regard to passers-by. Their opinions really don't matter and it's all too easy to find yourself providing an ear for any lonely soul who will see you as a sitting target.

It can help first to paint as part of a group. By having others around you, the public will spread their attention, thus taking the pressure off you. Also, in sharing the problem with others you will grow in confidence, knowing you are not alone.

Be careful to choose your spot carefully.

A very quick study using pen and waterproof ink overlaid with watercolour washes. Accents of white paper convey the effect of bright sunlight, which produces strong highlights on the water's surface and on the heads, shoulders and forearms of the figures.

strong sunlight against threatening sky

Slate roof patches of moss

Dark patches (Damp)

Foreground mainly ochre

You can tuck yourself away from the glare of the public, and protect yourself from hot sun, but make sure you haven't sacrificed an interesting viewpoint to create a good composition. It pays to spend a bit of time walking round your location to familiarise yourself with it, and to assess the best view point. Even then, sit for a while, perhaps with a coffee, to plan in your head what you want to achieve. What will be your centre of interest? Only then get your paints out and you will find you are less likely to make a compositional mistake.

With limited time, a limited palette is likely to be the best option. A pen and ink sketch

When making sketches for finished paintings, back up your drawing with written notes that help to describe specific colours and details, the time of day, the weather and light conditions.

Several quick sketches, even unfinished ones, can be as valuable as a single, involved study. They solidify your understanding of the overall structure and shapes of your chosen subject.

with just a little colour added at the end can produce a really lively result. Don't get bogged down in detail. Map in the bigger shapes and tonal structures, and just add suggestions of detail, or make smaller side sketches of these rather than finding you are unable to complete your overall study.

Be economic in what you take with you on your trip. Watercolour is ideal as it is one of the most portable media. Along with your paper or pocket sketchbook, you can just take a small box of paints, a couple of brushes, a pencil, and a bottle of water. An umbrella can also be useful for rain or sun, and plan your

clothing sensibly for sitting still for some time in possibly changeable weather.

Practical problems with painting itself include the fact that your light will change by the minute. You will probably need to work quite quickly, resulting in a series of quick loose studies rather than a grand finished piece. It can help to make notes on colour and atmosphere in case you want to work up your sketch later back at home.

Armed with a sketch pad and a soft pencil, you can make detailed studies of any interesting buildings or architectural features that you spot. These can later be included in a finished drawing or painting.

Figures in street scenes look more believable if they are engaged in some activity. Sketchbook studies, like this quick pen sketch of a motorcycle messenger, will provide you with a 'catalogue' of figures which you can incorporate into your townscapes.

When the crowds have gone home at the end of the day, the beach takes on a completely different aspect. This sensitive watercolour study was painted on a pre-stretched watercolour pad. Note how the dark, solid shapes of the groynes accentuate the luminosity of the sky and water.

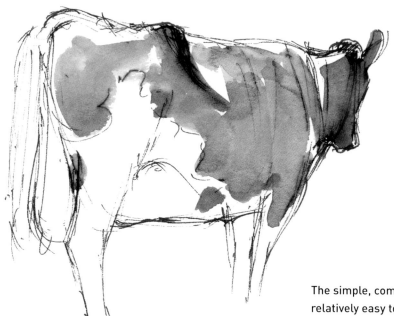

The simple, compact shape of a cow is relatively easy to draw. Note how the ink wash here conveys the bony prominence of the haunches.

Watercolour Landscape

*I*deally, landscapes should be painted on location rather than from photographs: a picture painted directly from nature has a freshness and an immediacy that cannot be reproduced in the studio.

Although watercolour is a spontaneous medium, you have to work methodically in order to keep your work fresh and lively; too much fiddling will result in muddy, overworked washes. Take time to plan the sequence of washes you are going to use and apply them quickly and decisively. Always work from light to dark: start by laying pale tones in thin, broad washes and work up to the dark tones with successive applications of thin layers of colour. Establish the large colour masses first, working broadly with the largest brush you can. Leave the detailed refinements till last, added with a smaller brush if necessary.

Working with a limited range of colour is not only practical for outdoor work – the less equipment you have to carry the better – it is also better for your painting as you will be more likely to achieve a harmonious colour balance. A variety of landscape greens, for instance, can be created mixing together just one yellow and one blue; by using more blue in the mix you make darker, cooler greens, and by using more yellow you make lighter, warmer ones. And because the same colours are repeated throughout, it helps to tie the image together and give it a satisfying unity.

[1] Tape a piece of Not surface watercolour paper to a board, or use a sketching block, and sketch out the composition very lightly with an HB pencil. It's best not to draw the outlines of the clouds as you want them to be soft, loose shapes. Then dampen the paper with clean water.

[2] Use a limited palette containing French ultramarine, lemon yellow, and raw sienna and a medium size round brush. Start by painting in the sky leaving ragged shapes for the clouds. Paint the undersides of the clouds using raw sienna. Note the perspective of the clouds, which appear darker, smaller and closer together as they near the horizon. Then block in the cornfield, trees and haystacks, mixing the ultramarine with the lemon yellow for the greens, and the raw sienna for the cornfield.

[3] Let the painting dry and then apply layers of stronger colour, gradually building up the forms with thin overlays. Use darker tones of green to model the forms of the trees and haystacks with shadow. Use the tip of the brush to add the finer details.

Tips on Landscape Painting

There are so many things to think about when painting a landscape, especially when on location, so here are just a few pointers and reminders to keep you on track. The main thing is to be inspired, and to translate the essence of the content and atmosphere onto your paper.

1. Just because it is there, you don't have to put it in! A landscape can seem overwhelming, so be selective. Think what you want to say in the painting. Is it about the atmosphere, the light, or the rhythm of the shapes? What will be your focal point? In doing this you will create a much stronger image.

2. Unless you are deliberately painting an accurate representation of a view, don't feel you have to slavishly paint exactly what's in front of you. If the composition works better by moving one or two elements around, or by introducing a completely imaginary one, then do it!

3. Create a definite focal point or focal area. Lead the viewer's eye around the picture space.

4. Get to grips with mixing greens. You can use some of the ready-mixed greens supplied by paint manufacturers, but nature contains such a wide variety that will change as light passes across the landscape, that you will need to experiment. Don't just stick with mixing blue and yellow either. You can create a much wider range by also adding siennas or black – play around with your palette.

5. Check your composition. Look at your painting in a mirror to check its composition. It will give you a completely different view on your work.

6. Assess your tonal range. Try scanning your painting on a flat-bed scanner, or photographing it digitally. On your PC transform it into black and white to analyse how your tonal range works. If you don't have a computer, you can photocopy it.

Reducing your image to black and white on a photocopier or scanner will immediately reveal your tonal range and balance.

Buildings

Whilst the countryside provides endless inspiration for atmospheric landscapes, towns and cities should not be overlooked for artistic potential. Buildings, whether rural or urban, each have a distinctive style that relates to their environment. In towns and cities, buildings and street scenes offer a readily accessible subject for sketching and drawing.

Walk down your local street and you will find a wealth of shapes, patterns and textures that provide the raw material for exciting pictures. There are many aspects to explore in the urban environment, from closely observed details of individual buildings to entire streets bustling with people and cars.

Different Types of Buildings

From your local town to an exotic holiday location, from farmyard to urban wasteland, man-made structures of all types are a continual source of inspiration and provide opportunities for creative drawing.

Making a detailed study of an individual building has a twofold reward: drawing skills are extended by exploring perspective, shape, form and tone, and a greater appreciation of the building itself is developed through the close observation required to draw it.

Whether in the town or the country, you are sure to come across an interesting building that inspires you to draw. There is no need to restrict yourself to drawing grand cathedrals, imposing mansions and picturesque cottages: ramshackle old buildings often have more potential than conventionally 'pretty' ones. Wrecks and ruins are fascinating subjects for creative interpretation because they have weathered and changed shape as parts of the original structure have fallen away, paint has peeled and stone has cracked. Modern buildings, too, make exciting subjects for pictures, with their bold geometric lines, shimmering glass facades and sky-scraping steel columns. With the industrial heritage of many cities, there are factories, petro-chemical plants, wharves, chimneys and cranes – not the most attractive structures, but you can make dramatic, moody tonal drawings of them or a delicate line-and-wash drawing will capture the play of light and shadow on an ornate facade.

Even in a simple pencil sketch, try to relate the building you are drawing to its surroundings. Here, vigorous hatching helps to tie together the windmill and the sky.

Many old buildings look as if they have grown naturally out of the landscape they sit in. Try to achieve a similar harmony in your sketches, using the same loose techniques for the building as for the landscape.

Ruined old farm buildings are often so well integrated into the landscape that they almost appear to be organic forms, like the surrounding hills and trees. In this watercolour study there is a harmonious interplay of textures: crumbling bricks, rusting corrugated iron and overgrown brambles.

Sketching Details

As well as complete buildings, it is rewarding to make sketches and studies on site of specific details, patterns and textures which you can use as a reference for a more considered painting back home.

Buildings are often rich with details that give them individual character and make them fascinating subjects to paint. With older buildings, in particular, features such as doors, windows, arches, balconies and architectural mouldings can make intriguing subjects in themselves. When you are walking around city streets, keep a sketchbook handy so you can jot down anything of interest. A simple pen or pencil will describe the delicate tracery of wrought iron gates and balconies with calligraphic lines; or you could use watercolour to record colourful verandas and shop awnings that create lively patterns within the overall framework of a shopping street.

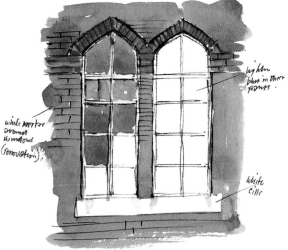

Careful study of the shadows creates solidity and monumentality in this small pencil sketch of an old stone doorway. Notice the gradation of the shadow inside the arch. Hold the pencil on its side for broad shading and use the point for picking out linear details.

Don't be too precise when drawing windows. Here, the edges of the colour washes don't follow the lines of the glazing bars exactly, and most of the glass panes are left unpainted, helping to integrate the window into its surroundings.

When you paint a street scene, it isn't necessary to define every window, brick and roof tile – a small area of texture can imply the whole. Broken brush strokes, dots and dashes will give an impression of intricate detail while gentle washes convey volume and solidity, and the play of light and shadow. With experience you will develop a kind of visual shorthand that suggests rather than labours over the details of buildings.

Pen and ink is a medium which is very effective in recording buildings and architectural details. As well as an overall sketch of the subject, you can make written notes about colours, tones and intricate details.

When a building is viewed from ground level, vertical perspective comes into play. Use your pencil to check the angles of the receding lines of roofs and chimney stacks.

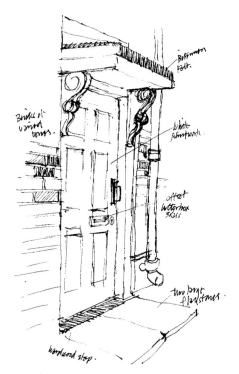

Many subjects suitable for detailed pencil work can be found on buildings. Here a 3B pencil records the intricate arrangements of bricks and tiles on the corner of a house.

A Building in Watercolour

An individual building can be a wonderful subject for a painting. Indeed people often commission artists to paint their house's 'portrait'. The challenge is to capture its character, function and relationship with its environment and the people who use it.

No matter how grand and imposing a building might be, its construction is still basically that of a cube, or a series of cubes. If you can draw a box in perspective, you can draw a building in perspective, and once you've got that right, the rest – doors, windows, chimneys, and balconies – will just fall into place.

Choosing a viewpoint

When a house is the main focus of interest in a picture it's important to show it to advantage and bring out its individual character. Walk around the site and find the best, most flattering angle of view. Decide whether you want to move in close, or include some of the surrounding scenery. The light is important, too, as shadows can help to explain forms and accentuate details and textures. As a rule it is best to avoid painting or drawing in the middle of the day, when the sun is high in the sky and casts minimal shadows. Most artists prefer early morning or late afternoon, when the sun casts long, descriptive shadows.

[1] Make a careful drawing of the house with a well-sharpened pencil. Start by lightly indicating the horizon line. Draw the vertical line at the front edge of the house. Draw the angles of the receding planes of the roof and extend these to the horizon line to fix the vanishing points on either side of the house. It is now a relatively simple task to complete the overall shape of the building and to establish the angles of the doors and windows. Then you can lightly indicate the landscape setting.

This house is viewed at a 45-degree angle, so two-point perspective comes into play. Two of its walls are visible, so there are two sets of perspective lines converging towards two vanishing points on the horizon line. As you can see from this picture, an oblique viewpoint enhances the scale and grandeur of the building and stresses its three-dimensional volume and solidity.

[2] Paint the sky and trees in the background and leave to dry before painting the main colours of the house. Then put in the foreground grass and flowers and the foliage along the front of the house. Allow the painting to dry.

[3] Suggest the window panes with tiny squares of medium and dark tone, leaving thin slivers of white for the glazing bars. Apply transparent dark washes over the shadow end of the house, under the eaves and beneath the windowsills. Suggest the pattern of the brickwork and add more detail to the foliage.

Still Life

Whether you intend to draw a still life for the sheer enjoyment of the shapes, as a study for a painting, or simply as an exercise, you will find that this accessible subject opens up many interesting possibilities, and poses many challenges. You may be tempted to draw an existing group of objects that you just 'happen' upon, or you can set up your own arrangement.

Many artists trawl thrift stores or auctions for inspiring objects or interestingly shaped pots, bottles and jugs, whilst nature provides a limitless source of subjects. You can gather flowers from the garden or florist, and build a collection of all kinds of items such as seashells, pine cones, rocks, or bones to study at your leisure back home.

Setting Up

A still life is one of the most straightforward subjects for the beginner. You can choose what objects make up the arrangement; to a large extent you are in control of the lighting; you won't get wet or frozen; and your subject won't move!

Setting up

When setting up a still life, don't be tempted to include too much. A few simple objects, selected for their qualities of shape, form and texture, will give you plenty to explore and enjoy.

Generally, still lifes work best when they have a kind of theme; one that has caught your attention and perhaps has a naturally harmonious composition or colour. For example, you might choose objects which are related through association – flowers and fruits, kitchenware and foodstuffs, plants and gardening implements being the most obvious examples. Or you might be drawn to particular objects for their pictorial qualities – shape, colour, tone, texture, pattern – and the contrasts and affinities they display when grouped together.

Consider the overall shape of the group you have arranged on the table. Look at it through a viewfinder and decide whether it fits more comfortably within a horizontal or an upright format. Here, for example, a fairly high viewpoint emphasises the vertical forces within the group and so an upright format is appropriate. The same group drawn in a horizontal format would be surrounded by too much empty space.

Composing the group

When you have arranged your still life, move around it and sketch it from different angles and viewpoints to see which makes the better composition. Each change of angle and viewpoint presents fresh possibilities, and you can extend those possibilities even further by using a viewfinder to home in on small sections of the group to create exciting 'cropped' compositions.

There is plenty to think about: does the light cast descriptive shadows that emphasise the form of the objects? Is there a reasonable variety of shapes and tonal contrasts? Examine the relationship not only between the objects themselves but the spaces between them as well; these 'negative' shapes should balance and enhance the 'positive' shapes of the objects, creating a cohesive design.

This group obviously fits more comfortably into a horizontal format. Try to arrange your still life in a way that emphasises the form and structure of the objects and the spaces between them. Study how each object relates to the others and be aware of spatial relationships. Small adjustments – moving an apple in front of a vase instead of next to it – will give a sense of depth to the drawing.

Textures and Details

The ability to convey texture is vital if you want your drawings to look realistic. Texture provides an opportunity to create decorative interest in a drawing that enlivens the overall composition.

When suggesting a particular texture, consider the full range of marks available to you: short, choppy strokes; nervous, wavy lines; small stippled dots; long curves and loops; even blurs, smears and spots. You can also create an illusion of texture by mirroring the tonal patterns that textures create and by bringing out the ways in which different surfaces reflect light.

Capture the hard, knobbly surface of a pineapple with heavy outlines, applying more pressure in the shadow areas. Hatch in each segment, modelling the tiny raised ridges with light and shade.

Glass reflects a lot of light, so use mostly pale tones and leave white paper for the sharp, bright highlights. Keep your shading as even as possible to convey the smooth glassy surface.

The graceful curve of a bird's feather is one of nature's marvels. Here the silvery tones and delicate marks made by a well-sharpened 2B pencil capture form and texture with a sensitive touch. Try drawing feathers with a fine-nibbed dip pen and sepia ink, too.

This coffee mill makes an attractive subject on which to practise drawing cubes and ellipses. The half-opened drawer adds interest to the drawing by breaking up the outline of the square base.

Crumpled paper forms stiff folds and distinct planes – qualities which you can bring out with hard contour lines and finely hatched shading in the shadow areas, leaving white paper for the sharp highlights.

Leaves and Petals

As you experiment you will see that some media and surfaces have inbuilt textural qualities that can be adapted to suit a particular subject. Charcoal dragged on its side across a coarse-grained paper will, for example, produce broken, textured marks that might suggest a rugged cliff face or a gnarled tree trunk. Ink wash on smooth paper lends itself naturally to conveying smooth glass and metal surfaces. Equally, though, you can render an animal's soft fur in pen and ink, or draw a delicate flower with charcoal – it's all in the handling.

Gather leaves from different tree species and record their different shapes and contours – smooth, toothed or lobed – in a sketchbook. Try to express the different textures of the leaves you have collected using hatching, cross-hatching and broad sweeps laid in with the side of the pencil.

Try using mixed media to capture the distinctive characteristics of flowers. Here, for example, the lily petals were washed in freely with watercolour and allowed to dry. The delicate striped markings were then picked out using coloured pencils.

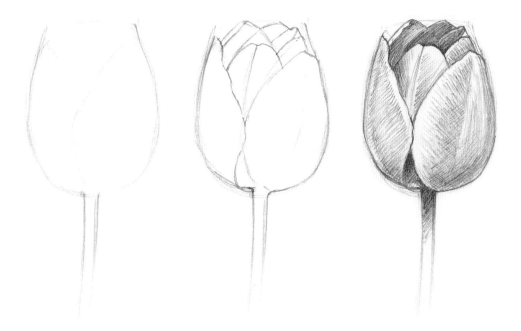

Start off by drawing flowers with simple, well-defined shapes, such as tulips. Using a 2B pencil, draw the outline shape with delicate, sketchy lines. Draw the inner petals, varying the strength of your pencil lines to convey the delicacy of the petals. Finally, make diagonal hatching lines to show the light and shade created both by the way the light falls on the flower and by the form of the flower itself.

The transparency of watercolour is ideal for the fragile forms of flower petals. Note where the lightest lights are and leave these as white paper. Before applying the first delicate wash, gently dampen the area to be painted with a fine brush. Apply increasingly darker tones to the flower while the underlying washes are still damp so that they merge to form subtle, translucent effects; if the paper is dry, the washes will dry leaving a noticeable line.

Still life in Watercolour

Still life is an excellent subject upon which to practise your painting and drawing skills in a similar way to how athletes use exercises to warm and tone muscles before a competition. It allows you to look at objects more closely, and just as importantly, the way that each shape works with another and creates interesting negative shapes.

With landscape, watercolour is the natural choice for its ability to create a fantastic range of atmospheric effects. In still life this has no importance, especially when the set up is on the kitchen table! As a result, throughout the history of art, watercolour hasn't been used very frequently for still life, with the exception of flower paintings where the transparent qualities suit the delicate textures and colours of petals. However, watercolour can very easily be employed for any kind of subject and its light, fluid application can lead to some intimate or spontaneous results.

Look out for ready made still lifes. A dining table, recently vacated, can create a wonderful narrative subject, as it yields suggestions of what has just taken place in the debris. So too can a pair of boots, kicked off after a walk or a game on the field. Collections of objects on a dressing table or in a hallway can speak volumes about their owners, and a quick sketch is best done in this medium.

[1] Set up a still life using objects in a range of sizes, shapes and textures. It's helpful to have some objects that are tall, and others squat to create a dynamic composition. Here the vinegar bottle echoes the curves of the onions and pepper, and adds height to what otherwise would be a dull composition. Note that it is placed off centre, again to create a more dynamic arrangement. Sketch out the contours lightly with an HB pencil.

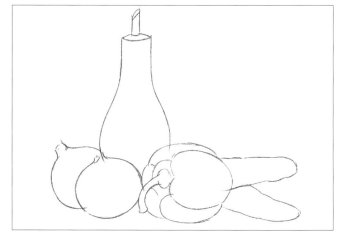

[2] Begin to add colour by applying light washes over the vegetables. The bottle, being the lightest part of the composition should be left as blank paper. Its contours can be defined by washing in a pale background. Here this has been achieved with a blue tint. The form of the objects can then be defined by adding further layers of colour to create shadows and the illusion of depth.

[3] To complete the painting, build up a rich depth of colour, using the shadows to show how each object is related to those around it. Make sure you add consistent highlights on the outward curves of the vegetables, and loosely suggest the texture of the onion skins. This can be achieved simply by letting colour run wet into wet.

People and portraits

Of all the subjects which an artist is likely to tackle, the human figure is undoubtedly the most challenging. If you can learn to draw faces and figures well, then you will be able to draw anything competently. It is not essential to have a thorough knowledge of anatomy in order to draw portraits and figures successfully. What is needed, however, as with any drawing subject, is a keen and analytical eye and a willingness to keep practising, even if your first attempts are unsuccessful.

Learning to interpret accurately the proportions of the body and at the same time instil a feeling of life into a figure is a real test of the artist's skill. Constant measurement and re-assessment while you work will help to ensure that your drawing is an accurate rendition of your subject, and this chapter offers practical advice on how to measure scale and proportion.

Proportion and Measurement

Figure drawing requires a higher degree of accuracy than most subjects. It doesn't really matter if the tree in your landscape drawing is slightly misshapen, but in a figure drawing, if the head is too small or the legs too short, it will be very noticeable. Practise is the key to getting the proportions of the human figure right, but fortunately there are also some simple rules to guide you.

The proportions of the body change as we grow and develop. The average adult body is approximately seven heads tall; a young child's body is about five heads tall and an older child's about six heads tall. These proportions provide a useful starting point but you will find that individual sitters often vary slightly from this average.

Proportions of the figure

It is helpful to know the proportions of the 'ideal' figure so that you can use them as a guide to accuracy when drawing people. Most artists use the head as a convenient unit of measurement. In a standing figure, the height of the head fits into the rest of the body approximately seven times.

The mid-point is not the waist, as is commonly assumed, but just above the crotch. With the arms by the side, the hands reach halfway down the thighs. The feet are generally about one head length long – a common mistake is to draw them too small. These are useful guidelines, but don't use them as a substitute for direct observation; few of us have perfectly proportioned bodies!

It's worth noting that many of the greatest artists have flouted the rules of proportion for stylistic effect. Cezanne's figures often have curious proportions, Matisse brazenly distorted the female form, and illustrators for the fashion industry deliberately draw figures with elongated bodies and small heads to create an impression of elegance.

Measuring

Use a pencil and your thumb to check the proportions of the figure as well as angles such as the slope of the shoulders or hips. Hold your pencil vertically, extend your arm fully, close one eye and look at the model. Align the top of the pencil with the top of the model's head and slide your thumb down until it aligns with the chin. Keeping your thumb in place and your arm fully extended, move the pencil to the measurement you want to check. Always hold the pencil at arm's length, with your elbow locked; if you bend your arm your measurements will be inaccurate.

When the weight is on one leg, the angle of the shoulders runs contrary to the angle of the hips so that the body balances itself. Drawing an imaginary vertical line down the centre of the body will help you to work out the variations in symmetry between the two sides of the figure.

Foreshortening is what happens when one part of a form is nearer to you than another. Here, the model's thighs are going away from the viewer and so appear shorter than they are in reality. If you look at the figure as a two-dimensional shape, you will find it easier to draw the foreshortened outline convincingly. Learn to trust what your eyes tell you! Use your pencil and thumb as a measuring tool to check key angles and proportions on the body.

Drawing the Head

When drawing portraits you will find it easier to achieve an accurate likeness if you have an understanding of the physical structure of the head and the proportions of the face.

Before tackling an actual portrait drawing, practise rendering some simple head shapes and learn how to position the features correctly in relation to the head. The basic form of the head is determined by the bony structure of the skull. This can be visualised

as an upside-down egg shape with the wider end representing the top of the head. Having established the shape of the head, you can position the features, and here the 'rule of halves' is a useful guide. First, draw a vertical line down the centre of the head to mark the position of the nose and the centre of the lips. Then draw a horizontal line across the centre of the head: this marks the position of the eyes and from here it is easy to gauge the eyebrow line. Sketch a line midway between the eyebrow line and the top of the chin in order to find the position of the base of the nose. Then draw a line midway between the base of the nose and the tip of the chin to find the line of the lower lip.

Now you can sketch the features. Allow for the gap between the eyes to be approximately the width of an eye. The ears line up between

The facial features occupy a surprisingly small area of the head. It is important to position them correctly in order to achieve a good likeness. Use the rule of halves as a rough guide to the position of the facial features.

the eyebrows and the tip of the nose. The hairline normally sits about one-third of the way down from the crown of the head.

Do bear in mind that the rule of halves is intended only as a guide to the 'average' face. Each individual is different and it is the variation from the norm that gives a face its distinctive character. Check proportions and relationships by measuring with your pencil.

When the head is tilted upward, downward, or to one side, the features appear foreshortened. As with the foreshortened figure, it can be difficult to accept these distortions until you learn to look at them logically.

When the head is lowered, the cranium appears larger and the shape of the face contracts. The steeper the angle of the head, the less of the face is visible. The features appear compressed. The tip of the nose may overlap the mouth and the ears are positioned higher than the eyes.

When the head is tipped backward, the eyes and nose appear much closer together. Notice how the facial features follow the curve of the underlying skull.

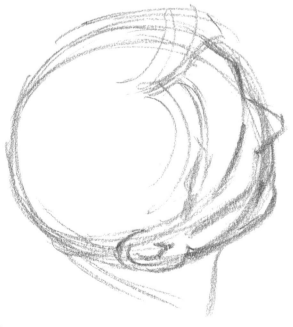

Informal Portraits

To develop your skills in figure and portrait work, why not start by making informal studies of your family and friends? Informal portraits are the artistic equivalent of a snapshot, in which the subject is dressed casually and adopts a relaxed and natural pose. They can be great fun to do, and the result, if successful, is a lively image that captures the personality of the sitter more readily than a formal portrait might.

If possible, persuade a friend or family member to pose for you for a couple of hours at least. This will give you plenty of time to try out different poses and make preliminary sketches. When setting up your model you need to find a position that is comfortable for him or her, and one that creates an interesting shape. In this pose the model is sitting down with the legs drawn up and the arms in a comfortable position. This creates a relaxed, natural pose that is also visually pleasing: the varied angles of the legs and arms set up a series of rhythms that give life and animation to the drawing and lead the eye around the picture.

Foreshortening

Perspective makes things appear to shrink as they recede, so that if you look at a seated model from the front you will see that the thighs appear compressed in length. Foreshortened shapes can appear extreme and you may want to alter them to make them more recognisable. But you must force yourself to draw what you see, not

[1] Sketch in the main outlines of the figure with a 6B pencil. Hold the pencil loosely, well back from the point, and make light, tentative marks – hard outlines make the figure look wooden. Avoid too much rubbing out; when mistakes occur, leave them in and draw the more accurate lines alongside. These re-stated lines give life to the drawing.

what you know. To help you get the shapes and proportion right, use the pencil-and-thumb method described on page 71. You might also like to make a quick sketch before you begin your drawing.

Start by sketching in the overall outline of the figure with fluid lines, making sure that it will fit comfortably on the page. Draw with

your whole arm, not just your fingers. Only when you have something resembling the pose should you return to specific areas and start to tighten them up.

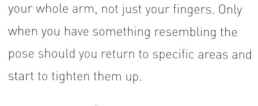

[2] Once you are happy that the outline of the figure is accurate, rub out the guidelines and start to tidy up the drawing – though still avoid making hard outlines. Indicate the positions of the facial details and the outline of the hair. Start to emphasise the important lines, making them heavier where they project forward and lighter where they recede.

[3] Half close your eyes so that you can see the areas of light and shadow. Apply loose hatching to the shaded areas of the face and limbs. This will make the figure appear more solid and three-dimensional. Finally, apply more pressure with the pencil to add dark tones to the hair, sweater and shoes.

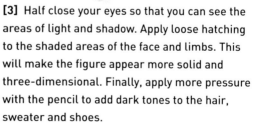

The Figure in Watercolour

Adding colour to your sketches can bring them to life. Although you can paint very detailed images in watercolour, it is particularly good for quick sketches. You can capture friends or family in natural poses as they go about their daily business, or ask them to adopt a specific pose.

Try to relax as you approach a painting. If you are tense, you will produce a stiff, lifeless image, and your tension may well transfer to your sitter. Remember that sketching can be like a warming up exercise. It limbers you up, focuses your mind, but since you are not producing a finished painting, the process and practise is more important than the result. It can be very beneficial to work as part of a group. If there are a number of you, you could share the cost of booking a professional model to work with. Whoever you use, your model must be comfortable or they will be unable to hold a pose. Give your sitter a fixed point to look at, such as a picture on the wall, so that the position of the head and eyes

Begin with an outline drawing in pencil. You may have to alter and correct the drawing several times before you are ready to paint, so use a soft pencil and draw with light pressure. Avoid too much rubbing out as this spoils the surface of the paper.

Dampen the figure and chair with clean water and brush in the main areas of colour quickly, using as large a brush as you can. Treat the hair as one overall mass, then suggest the curls and tresses with curved strokes.

remains constant. Remember that frequent breaks are essential. Before a break, use masking tape or chalk to mark the position of feet, hands and elbows on the floor and chair so that he or she can regain, as near as possible, the exact pose after the break.

Give some thought to the position of the figure on the paper. The head should not be so close to the top of the page that it looks cramped, or so far down that the figure seems to be slipping out of the picture. Don't necessarily place the figure in the centre of the sheet: the spaces which are left empty around it are all part of the complete composition, helping to suggest the space in which the figure sits.

Make a brief pencil sketch to establish a guideline at the start, but allow the image to develop freely by drawing over the pencil lines with the brush. When you begin the sketch, start with the broad areas of colour and tone which describe the main shapes and forms of the figure. Leave details such as the facial features till the end and don't worry about achieving a likeness. The vitality of this type of study depends upon working quickly with fluid and vigorous brushwork. Let the paint dry completely from time to time so that subsequent colour washes are fresh and sharp. Small linear details such as the eyes and mouth can be drawn over a dry wash with the tip of the brush.

At this stage you can apply darker washes to describe the shading on the face and hair and the creases and folds in the clothing. Try not to overwork the colours. Leave small areas of paper untouched to suggest highlights on the skin and hair. Touch in the features deftly using the fine tip of the brush.

Sketchbook Studies

*I*t's a good idea to get into the habit of carrying a pocket sketchbook around with you, in order to make lots of rapid sketches of figures as often as you can.

Regular sketching is the best way to learn how to portray figures convincingly, so get out and about and sketch people in everyday situations as often as you can. Find a suitable location where people tend to congregate and linger, such as cafés and restaurants, train stations, museums, and art galleries. At the beach or in the local park, people walking dogs, playing games, or sitting on benches provide ample models. Stores and markets, sports arenas, and construction sites offer the challenge of sketching moving figures. The possibilities are endless.

Drawing in public places calls for courage and self-confidence, but with a pocket-sized sketchbook and a simple pen or pencil tucked in your pocket, a sketch can be made in a few minutes, even a few seconds, and it can be

Choose a spot where your subjects are unaware that they are being sketched, allowing you to catch lively expressions and movements.

done discreetly. You don't have to think in terms of making a finished drawing, just jot down what you see at a glance. Keep things small and simple. Speed is of the essence, so try to grasp the essentials – the overall shape, posture, and action of the figure. Don't be discouraged if your first attempts are inaccurate or too tight – the more you do, the more intuitive your drawings will become.

Bars are an excellent source for characters, expressive gestures and incidental details. This sketch was drawn with waterproof ink and watercolour wash.

A journey on public transport need not be boring if you carry your sketchbook with you. Trains, buses, and aeroplanes are great places for people-watching, and if you manage to draw discreetly and catch people unawares, you can produce marvellous character studies.

A quick, spontaneous sketch can often be more incisive and expressive than a highly finished drawing because it captures the essentials of character and gesture.

Sketching Children and Babies

Sketches and drawings are a wonderful way to capture those precious moments of childhood that are over all too soon. But you have to learn to be 'quick on the draw'!

Drawing young children is always a challenge because they never keep still for long. Start off gently by drawing a child asleep, or absorbed in a favourite book or TV programme. At least you will stand half a chance of getting something down on paper! When you feel brave enough, progress to sketching children on the move. The secret is speed and practice. If you have children at home, keep your drawing materials readily to hand and try to make at least one sketch of them every day. Your pace of drawing will increase and you will begin to develop methods of rapid notation that enable you to catch a fleeting pose or expression.

As children move about and play, make several sketches on a single sheet and dart from one to the other. Put down your impressions with simple, unfussy strokes and concentrate on the outline shapes and gestures of the figures – don't worry unduly about details such as faces and hands.

Selecting a medium

To capture the charm and innocence of children, and their energy and enthusiasm, you will need a medium that is both rapid and sensitive. Soft pencil is a good 'instant'

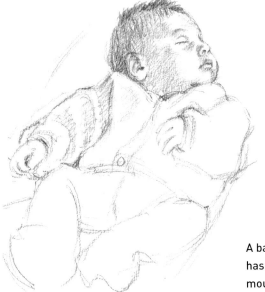

A baby has a very large head in comparison to its body. It has very rounded, large cheeks and the eyes, nose and mouth are crowded into a small area of the face.

medium that can also be smudged with a finger for soft tones. Very quick sketches can be made by smudging soft pastel or charcoal to catch the overall shape of the pose, then drawing in the details with the point of the stick. Gentle watercolour washes are perfect for delicate sketches of babies and young children. The contours of the face and body are much softer in children than in adults, so modelling should be kept broad and simple.

These simple pencil sketches capture the charm and innocence of young children at play. Making quick, sketchy drawings of moving children helps to develop your speed and confidence so that you are better able to capture something of the energy and vitality of your subjects.

Here, delicate watercolour washes over light pencil outlines create an appealing and lifelike sketch of a young toddler. The pose – head turned, one leg slightly raised – implies movement and energy.

A Portrait in Watercolour

Watercolour is an excellent medium for spontaneous, informal portrait studies. Its fluidity and translucency are perfectly matched to the subject, bringing out the delicate, living qualities of skin and hair.

The secret of sketching portraits in watercolour is to work systematically and confidently, keeping your washes as clear and fresh as possible. Inexperienced painters often make the mistake of using the paint too thickly and overworking the skin tones, with the result that the skin appears muddy and lifeless. The beauty of watercolour is that delicate, transparent washes allow light to reflect off the white paper beneath, creating an impression of the skin's natural luminosity.

In keeping with traditional watercolour practice, always start with very pale, diluted colours and gradually strengthen the tones with successive washes laid one over the other. It is important to keep the colours bright and fresh: you need to use plenty of clean water and rinse your brushes thoroughly after each colour application. Try not to 'muddy' the image with too many colours and keep reworking to a minimum to maintain the delicacy of the washes.

The skin appears lighter and warmer in the prominent light-struck areas, such as the cheeks and forehead, and darker and cooler in the shadow areas. Because warm colours appear to advance and cool

[1] Make a light pencil drawing of the model, carefully studying the relative proportions. In this pose the arm is nearer than the face and so appears large in comparison. When the drawing is complete, rub out any unwanted lines, leaving an image that is clear enough to guide the painting but doesn't interfere with the delicate washes of watercolour.

colours to recede, you can use these warm and cool contrasts to model the contours of the face and figure, much as a sculptor pushes and pulls a block of clay. In this portrait, for instance, notice the warm yellows on the cheek, the chin, and the bridge of the nose, and the subtle hints of cool blue in the shadows of the face and arm.

[2] Dampen the figure with water and block in the palest flesh tones. Model the contours of the face, arm and hair with successive washes of darker, cooler colours. Keep the paint fluid and allow the colours to merge on the damp paper to suggest the softness of the flesh.

[3] Apply your colours with confidence and do not attempt to tidy up the loose brush strokes too much – the portrait will look much more lively if you allow some of the brush marks and ragged edges to show rather than blending them neatly together.

[4] Strengthen the colours over the whole image, developing the structure of the face and arm with a series of overlapping washes. Define the tresses of hair with curving brush strokes, letting the pale underwash show through to suggest highlights and individual wisps of hair. Define the eye and mouth with dark colour applied with the tip of the brush.

Animals

Animals and birds are sometimes frustrating but always fascinating subjects to draw. Their feathers, scales and fur provide a wealth of patterns and textures to explore with a range of media and techniques. Recording their characteristic behaviours, their gestures and movements, will test your skills of observation and mark-making.

Drawing animals and birds presents a problem similar to that of drawing young children – they cannot be asked to pose for you, so you will have to rely on preliminary sketches and a good background knowledge of the underlying structure of the animal. Start by drawing your own pet, which is more likely to keep still for you. If you find that you develop an interest in this subject, you can go on to study the animals and birds on farms, in zoos and in the wild.

Basic Shapes

*I*f you are serious about drawing animals you need to develop a knowledge of how they move and generally behave. We don't think twice about this when drawing people, since we automatically know how we work. Watch natural history documentaries, and start by drawing from photographs before progressing to drawing your pet.

As with any subject, you can start by simplifying the form of the animal in front of you. Look for the basic underlying shapes: from the side, a cat's head forms a roughly oval shape and the ears are small, elongated triangles. A dog's head fits into a square or hexagonal shape, depending on the breed, and the body is shaped like a kidney bean. All animals can be visualised as a series of simple, interlocking geometric shapes – circles, ovals, triangles, and rectangles. Once you are familiar with the basic shapes of animals, you will find it easier to sketch them from life, with fluid lines and rhythmic gestures that capture their grace and movement.

Simple outline drawings like these are fun to create. They show how it is possible to draw the basic body structure of any animal, large or small, by seeing it as a collection of interlocking geometric shapes. Side views are the simplest to start with.

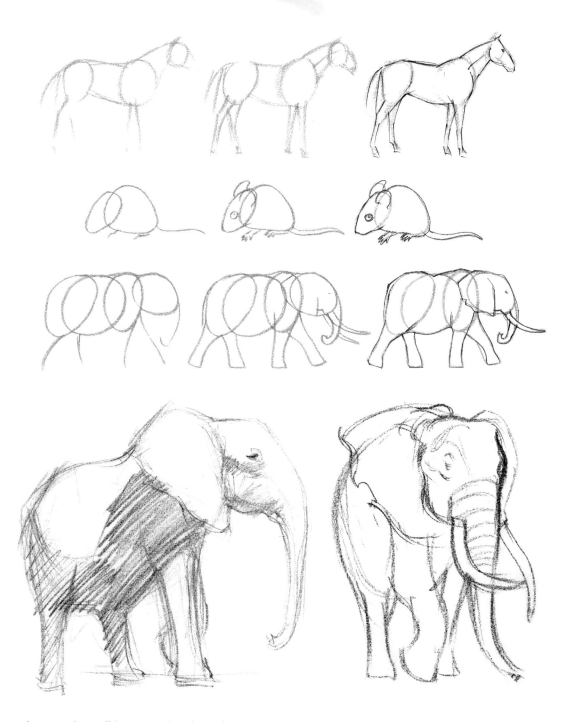

As you gain confidence, try drawing animals on the move. Watch them carefully to feel how their entire bodies move, and still working with your basic shapes, try to find the lines that sum up the movement.

Sketching Animals

Animals don't keep still for long, so quick sketches are important resources for larger paintings. Family pets make the best models since they are always around and you can make studies of them sleeping, eating or gazing out of the window.

Start by sketching your cat or dog sleeping. This gives you the chance to learn about structure and proportions, which will enable you to draw a moving animal quickly and accurately. Next, try sketching your pet while grooming, it will remain fairly stationary but perform a series of repeated movements, which will allow you to record the rhythmic grace of the pose. Have several sketches of different poses on the go at once, and dart around the page as your subject shifts position. This is quite a challenge but you should end up with a page of interesting studies.

Proportions are important in capturing the individuality of your pet. The big ears, long tail, and gangly limbs tell us that this is a puppy.

Mice, hamsters, and gerbils are lively little animals. The speed and suddenness of their movements make them hard to draw – you just have to sketch rapidly as they skitter about. This sketch was done with an ink pen and then washed over with watercolour.

This portrait of a tabby cat is worked in soft graphite pencil. The eyes are the key to the character and expression of an animal. This applies particularly to cats, whose eyes are such a prominent feature. Start your drawing by checking the size and position of the eyes in relation to the other features of the head.

A black Conté pencil held on its side produces soft tones that describe the sleek, smooth and muscular forms of rabbits. Working on a coarse-textured paper helps to give a suggestion of softness to the coat.

Watercolour is a good medium for conveying the texture of fur if you simplify the furry texture into broad areas of tone rather than attempting to paint each hair. Apply quick, directional brush strokes over an almost-dry underwash to suggest the thick, rug-like fur on the dog's body.

Details and Textures

The textures, colours and patterns of fur, feathers and scales are a rewarding area of study when drawing animals. Try to find marks that will represent them with conviction, but without overstatement.

When you are drawing animals and birds you will find that their patterns and markings can help to describe the underlying form. The stripes of a tiger or a tabby cat, for instance, follow the contours of the body and give it a feeling of solidity. Your first priority, however, is to get down the structure and proportions of the body. Only when you have got the shape and pose right should you start to tackle details and patterns.

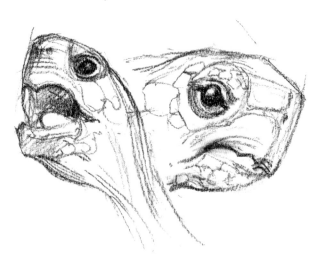

When drawing the scaly skin of reptiles, a feel for the rhythm of the markings will be more characteristic than the minute reproduction of every detail.

Coloured pencils were used here to portray the hamster's sleek, velvety, colourful fur with short, fine lines that follow the contours of the form. The tiny highlights on the eye are important in conveying their brightness.

It is essential to find a quick, shorthand way of describing an animal's texture or coat pattern. If you try to draw every spot, stripe, hair, or feather your drawings will look lifeless and overworked. Observe where the most distinctive markings are and use them to emphasise the shape of the animal in key places such as around the head, shoulders and rump. The eye fills in the gaps, so a few carefully placed marks are read as a complete pattern or group of hairs.

Be expressive with your mark-making to bring out the character of a texture. Short fur can be imitated with hatched lines; the tonal gradations across the body built up by varying

It is possible to capture the formidable beauty of a large bird of prey in a zoo, where the confined situation encourages the birds to sit still for long periods of time. Watercolour is a suitable medium for recording detailed impressions, conveying the bird's bulk and the structure of feathers with delicacy and freedom.

the density and pressure of the marks. Draw animals with long, smooth hair using broad areas of tone with occasional lines to suggest the rhythms of its fall. Pay attention also to the shadows and highlights on the fur or feathers as they help to describe the structure of the body beneath.

The complex whorls and ridges on a tortoise's shell are a delight. However, you don't have to reproduce each individual scale. In this study, watercolour washes were used to suggest the patterns with a 'lost and found' quality that implies their continuation around the creature's form.

A Stag in Watercolour

For a painting of a wild animal like this stag, you will probably need photographic reference for both the animal and the context in which it is found. You might be lucky to make sketches at a zoo or in parkland. Try to do this if you can.

Drawings and paintings made from photographic reference tend to be tighter than those produced spontaneously, but in using photographs you can study detail that you would not normally get the chance to as an animal swiftly moves past. If you are doing a more formal painting, it adds interest to place your subject in its natural context. If you become serious about a particular type of animal, study their habitat and make lots of sketches and paintings to provide you with a range of backdrops. Watch the animals to see if they move together in herds or prefer to stand alone. This will add authenticity to your work.

In this image the stag is set against a mountain background which provides a more dynamic backdrop than a flat landscape. The mountain complements the height of the stags antlers and the form of the landscape has been used to create new shapes under the body of the animal.

[1] Sketch in the contours of the animal in a soft pencil. Think about the background and how you might break up what might otherwise be areas of empty space. The mountain balances the overall shape of the stag whilst setting the head against the open sky serves to draw the eye to it, which is, in any case, the focus of interest.

[2] Wash in the background using the wet in wet technique. The sky can be created by leaving areas of white paper, and also dropping in touches of yellows and siennas to suggest more dramatic conditions. Suggest shadows under the animal with deeper washes of green, and then add a wash of burnt sienna over the stag as a base colour. Ensure that you reserve the highlights around the eyes, mouth and ears.

[3] Define the form of the stag by building up layers of siennas and umbers, trying to create your darkest colours from mixes rather than black which will deaden your painting. Add details such as the eyes and nostrils with a finer brush once you are satisfied with the balance of colour and tone across the painting.

Tips on Painting Animals

Animals can be such exciting subjects to paint, and it is just as important to capture their character as it is when painting people. The more you understand the structure, movement and behaviour of a species, the better your painting will be. Check through the following points before you begin.

1. Start by making quick sketches. Accept the fact that your pet will probably move just as you are working on a particularly challenging aspect of their fur or structure. Don't get cross otherwise your pet will pick up on your tension and never settle.

2. Take reference photographs. Although it's best to work directly from the animal, photographs take some of the pressure off as you will then have clear reference material. By using your photos as well as looking at the animal, whatever pose they might ultimately take up, you will gain a better understanding of the structure and texture and produce a better image. Keep simply watching your pet – it will enhance that deep knowledge of how the skeleton and muscles work.

3. Analyse the direction and patterning of the animal fur. It will help you understand the structure of the animal underneath. If you get the direction of the hair wrong, you will not be able to create a convincing image. Look carefully before you start drawing.

A quiet grooming session at the zoo offered the chance to sketch these two young friends in pencil and watercolour, concentrating on the faces and suggesting the bodies with loose outlines.

4. Create a sense of individuality. Pet owners know the characteristics of their animals. Don't paint to a formula. Study the pet, get to know their character, and try to communicate this in your drawing, just as you would in a human portrait.

5. Study the anatomical structure of the animals you choose to paint. It will really help you understand how the limbs bend and join to the body. It is often very hard to get the legs of animals right as they are often on the move, and hidden by fur. Check out zoology books and photographs before you make your studies, and really get to grips with your subject.

6. Depending on the species of animal, the tail is an indicator of mood. Be very careful not to make it look as if it is just stuck on! It's an extension of the spine, and can be an elegant counter for balance or a fly swat. Make sure you allow it to make its own statement.

7. Suggest the scale. We all know that an elephant is huge, and a mouse, tiny, but there are all kinds of species that we don't know so well, or breeds of animals whose sizes will vary enormously. It is helpful, therefore, to include something in your painting to indicate the scale. You might want to add a zoo keeper sweeping out an enclosure, a bone, or a detail of a building or plant.

8. Think about your viewpoint. Just because we look at animals from a particular orientation or vantage point, it doesn't mean you have to paint the animal from that angle. What about taking a mouse's eye view and paint your cat huge and from beneath, or a view of a cow from the water trough, just before its nose is about to dive in. You will get a much more interesting composition.

This watercolour sketch of a gazelle concentrates on the elegant head, with its beautiful ridged horns and huge dark eyes. Delicate washes of colour help to capture the animal's gentle expression.

Index